What Others Are Saying

THE MIDWEST BOOK REVIEW

". . . Every novel, regardless of its genre, needs to open with a hook, and then irresistibly propel the reader to dive in and become immersed in the story from beginning to end. ROBIN by Kenneth Shelby Armstrong is just such a novel and highly recommended as an original and carefully crafted story from first page to last."

James A. Cox, Editor-in-Chief

Marilyn A. Hudson

Armstrong's "Robin" Soars High.

"Oklahoma author Kenneth Shelby Armstrong presents a story of lyrical beauty, deeply felt emotion, thought provoking actions, and lasting inspiration."

Marilyn A. Hudson Reviewer

"An interesting, even compelling collection. Some of the essays have phrases that have that lasting impact worth repeating, rising to the level of superb writing."

T. W. Jones, attorney at Law
Colorado Springs, Colorado

"Armstrong shows unusual insight into his subject and has the literary skill to express it forcefully and meaningfully"

Val J. Christensen, Ph.D.
Educator, San Diego, California

"I read your book in one sitting. It is truly a fine piece of work. . . Your writing is superb."

James D. Hamilton,Ed.D.
Psychologist,
Austin, Colorado

"Great project! I've never seen a similar one."

Forrest Ladd, Ph.D.
University Vice President

"The wit, wisdom and wealth of words that powerfully communicate from your soul to ours, is a gift and anointing I've known of you for 55 years. Keep it up."

Walter Thomas, Ed.D.
Educator, Speaker, Motivater

"Fascinating experience, and one that I did not know you had! Indeed your life seems to unfold into a story book of rich adventures, each a puzzle piece in a most dynamic, influential and inspirational life!"

Vivian Stewart
Poet, Author, Artist, Creator

I have so enjoyed reading these four books by a local, very intelligent, gifted writer in our community...Dr. Kenneth Armstrong...I would encourage you all to partake in his history by purchasing them on Amazon.. his stories are amazing.

Sean Boone, D.O.
Hugo, Oklahoma

Win With Wisdom Series

ksa

Kenneth Shelby Armstrong Th.D., Ed.D.

Copyright © 2017

"It's WISE To Know The Big Picture"

The strategies of *Getting by Giving*

Kenneth Shelby Armstrong Th.D., Ed.D.

"It's WISE To Know
The Big Picture"

The strategies of *Getting by Giving*

The Tax Code of the Internal Revenue Service is greatly generous in one respect. It lets us keep 10% of our annual earnings if we will give it to charity. The rest if our earnings are subject to attack from local, State, National taxes and everyone else. But most people want to keep as much of their earnings as they can.

Getting as much as you can and keeping as much as you can is an ancient principle and the preoccupation of the average person. I'm not sure that it is something taught to the young, for I remember that it was ingrained in my children before we taught them anything.

The word "Mine" is one of the first words that children learn. And without any coaching from others they learn the skills of "getting" what they want. Crying, tantrums, pouting, and like behavior is mastered and used as long as they can get by with it.
Indeed I have known many adults who still use these techniques to get what they want.

There seems to be no limit to "wanting." It is a malady that chases us all of our lives. And the lack of getting what we want is the cause of more wasted lives, more lost opportunities, more fractured relationships and more personal sufferings than we can imagine. Still, we pursue our cravings and desires to the detriment of our true best interests.

My father had a saying and I remember it to this day.

"Some folks have a philosophy of getting all they can, canning all they get, and sitting on the lid."

But there is a strangeness to this "wanting" phenomenon. In many/most cases the satisfaction of our desires do not make us any happier, or better off.

But we never learn that fact. We keep wanting things—both good and bad.

Now, is that a bad thing? Should we attempt to kill those desires and urgings? The answer does not lie in their destruction, but rather in **facing** them in the context of our callings in life.

Desires are like horses. They are best used when harnessed to a task. But, of course, most people have not adopted an important task in life so there is nothing to harness. And if you do not have a purpose—you are vulnerable to the lures and temptations of desires.

Actually, the issue is one of how we will live our lives. It is important to discover the principles that govern these urgings and ultimately our lives. And who will teach us these principles? Do we have to wait until retirement to finally learn how we should react to these issues? Hopefully not! Life has placed in our paths, teachers from out of nowhere to open our eyes. Let me tell you how this happened to me.

I was president of a small college that had more wants and needs than any institution that you have ever seen. Most of the time the greatest need was a little thing like— MONEY. But no matter how much money came in, there was still an encyclopedia of needs, and it was the president's job of finding the money somewhere.

One day one of the college's supporters came into my office and said "Do you need any money?" He immediately got my attention, but as I looked at his attire and bearing I quickly judged that this was just another rabbit to chase, but I politely asked him if he had an idea where we could get some.

He grinned broadly and replied that he knew a very rich man down in Florida who had lots of money and liked to give it away to worthy projects. He said he had the man's telephone number and if I would call and talk to him, he would probably give me an appointment.

Without much enthusiasm I took the telephone number and put it on my desk. I thanked the supporter for thinking about us and promised him that I would follow through on the prospect.

As I went about my daily tasks that piece of paper kept looking at me accusingly. The days passed and I could take it no longer. I called the man. Friendly? Yes, he was very friendly —what more could you want?

And yes he would like to see me. We set the date and I put the telephone number in my wallet where I would not lose it.

Now my next task was to develop my speech to the man when I got there. For the next couple of days I thought about nothing but what I should say. How much I should ask for? What should we do with the money? I really wanted that money.

I used my credit card and got a round trip ticked to Fort Lauderdale, Florida. I arrived the evening before my morning meeting. I wanted to be fresh and fully rehearsed for the occasion. To be honest I didn't get much sleep that night.

I was already awake when the alarm went off. I jumped out of bed and went into the bathroom to get ready. I had rented a car the night before so I could get to his place on the beach. I didn't have much of an appetite so breakfast didn't take long.

I drove to the address and arrived early. I parked behind some trees in front of his house so he wouldn't know that I was out there. Five minutes before the appointment I got out of the car and walked down a lane that led to his house. I knocked on the door, but I really didn't need that to tell him I had arrived. My heart was beating loud enough to let the whole neighborhood know that I had arrived.

Mr. Carmen Adams came to the door, opened it with a great smile and asked me to come in. As I walked into the room I saw a bank of windows stretching from one side of the room to the other side, and from the floor to the ceiling. And, beyond the windows was a wide beach and the waves were coming in and rolling up the beach and then rolling back to the huge Atlantic ocean. The sight was striking as was the large room and the magnificent furnishings.

He offered me a seat on a sofa facing the beach and moved to his seat which was surrounded by books, magazines and papers. I could tell that this man was not retired—he was still engaged in business and a busy life.

He was very cordial and we talked about his home and its location right on the beach. He asked me a few question about where I came from and where I had gone to school. The conversation was pleasant and not hurried at all, but finally he asked, "What can I do for you?"

I immediately went into my well-rehearsed spiel about the college and our needs. I didn't talk long and when I finished, I quit talking.

He was looking out at the ocean when I finished, but he didn't say anything for a very long time. I was nervous. He didn't ask any questions. He didn't make any comments. I felt like I was at a funeral, and someone that I loved dearly had died.

Finally he said "Well, I'm not going to give you any money. I wish I could, but you don't fit my criterion. I only give to certain causes and yours is not one of them. I wish I could help you out, but I just can't."

Strangely, he didn't move or get up. He just sat there and looked at me in sort of a sad way. Since he had not moved, I couldn't move. I was not sure that I could make it to the door even if I could get up. And then he spoke again.

"Dr. Armstrong, I already know a lot about your college and I am sure you are doing a good job, and perhaps someday I will be able to give you a gift. But right now I can't give you money, but maybe—just maybe—I can give you something that will be more useful than money. I can give you some advice."

My heart sank again. **Advice!** I didn't need advice. I got advice every day from faculty, students, board members, alumni, big donors —everyone wants to give me advice—but I need money.

In spite of the way that I felt inside, I smiled and said "That would be nice. Thank you."

"When I was your age, I hadn't yet learned that there were two games in town. I didn't know that there were **two**. I had only been taught that there was **one** game, and I learned to play it very well. I wish I had known about the other game when I was young. It would have made life much easier."

"What do you mean that there are two games in town?" I asked.

"Don't feel bad about it. I was in my late fifties when I learned this great secret. You are still young and have a long time to find out about what I call a **secret**. I think that you could learn it a lot faster than I learned it if you put your mind to it."

Curiosity got the better of me and before I thought, I blurted out: "What's the secret?"

"It's the *give* and **get** secret. Some people call it the *push—pull* secret. The only game that I knew about was the *get* or *pull* game. Here's how it works.

"In a business transaction you try to *pull* all you can out of the deal. If you can get more out of the deal than your opponent, you win. If you don't out-pull your opponent, you lose.

"In a company setting, you try to pull more money out of your boss. You try to get more time off. You try to get a long vacation. You are alway 'pulling' but so is your boss, and he can usually out-pull you.

"If you play that game all of your life, when you get 65 or 70 you look at your assets and discover that LIFE has out-pulled you and you will have barely enough to survive. That is so sad because if you had chosen to play the push game, LIFE would have out-pushed you and you would have plenty. It's all about what game you want to play.

"If you choose to play the **pull** game you will find out that LIFE is so much stronger than you and it will out-pull you. You probably will lose. If you learn to play the **push** game, LIFE will play that game too and it will push to your coffers with more than you ever dreamed of getting."

"I still don't understand." I countered.

"Let me explain. A few months ago a young man came through that door and told me that he had a great idea for a good business. He had tested it and it worked. He drew up a business plan and it was good.

"He said he was looking for finance. He told me how much he needed and explained how much I could make. He said he would do all of the work and be responsible for making the business a success. For doing that he wanted 50% of the business and a small salary from the business.

"He said all I would have to do is provide the cash for the venture and lend my advice to the operation.
He said that a 50/50 split seemed to be fair, and I agreed with him. I told him that he had a deal and to get his lawyer to draw up the papers.

"A couple of weeks later he called and said the papers were done and ready for signature. I told him to come right over and we would complete the deal.

"They came and we got ready to sign them. I looked the papers over and said, wait a minute, I'm not too happy with one thing and I want to change it before I sign. The lawyer protested. 'But we had a deal.'

"I told him I was aware of that, but I wanted to make one change. I told him I didn't like that 50/50 split. I told him I wanted to change it to a 60/40 split. Well the lawyer objected. His face got beet-red He countered by saying that we had a deal and I couldn't change the split provision. I told him that if we didn't change that split to 60/40 I wouldn't sign.

"The young man who was to be my partner looked white in his face—ashen. He was scared. So I said son, I do want to change the split to 60/40, but I want you to have the 60 and I will take the 40. I told him that he was inexperienced and a lot of things could happen that he had not thought of and if he had a bigger split he would have a better chance of being more successful.

"I told him 'look I'm already rich and if this doesn't work out it will not hurt me at all.

However since you don't have money to get you through an unexpected problem you could loose everything and it would hurt you and your family. That's why I want to change the split.'

"Now this explains the miracle. Since I play the push game I am always pushing as much as I can to the other fellow. He can see that and he will always want to do business with me. And my secret gets around.

"Now anytime there is a great deal being developed in Southern Florida, the owners often will want to do business with me because they know I will always act to protect their best interests first, even before I protect my own. Everybody wants to do business with old Carmen, because I will always **push** the deal towards them and not **pull** towards me.

"And, I just sit here looking out at the ocean, and people come in the door and make me rich. If I played the **pull** game, I wouldn't get all these deals, because people know if I wanted to play the **pull** game I could out-pull them. That's how the push game is played and anyone who will truly play it can get rich and have all their needs met."

I said, "That's amazing. Could I learn how to play it?"

"Sure you can. When you came through that door this morning you were thinking 'I wonder how much I can get out of old Carmen. I saw that you wanted to play the **pull** game, so I **out-pulled** you. If you had been saying I wonder what I can give to Carmen? Or what could I do or say or give to him that he doesn't have but he needs? If you had been thinking that, I would have known it and would have played that game with you. And you would have been leaving here with a nice large check.

"Trust me Dr. Armstrong, if you will change your mind-set to **giving** or **pushing**, you will never be a loser. I have just told you the **secret**. Now go out and put it to work. I think your Bible says 'Give and it will be given to you, pressed down and running over.' You're a smart fellow. Go out and be a giver."

Well, it was the biggest gift that I had ever received and I could see that in a strange way it made perfect sense, but I wasn't sure how it would work in a practical setting. I knew that theories were great, but if they didn't work in the real world, they wouldn't help much. So much to think about

Some Parables

Two young men applied for jobs with a local business that was growing and it looked like it would be a successful venture. They both were hired and their prospects looked good. But it didn't take long for them to become aware that they were in competition for advancement. It wasn't cut-throat competition, but it was a serious factor in their futures.

Chad was a little older than Barry and had a little more experience than the younger man. He was good looking and several inches taller. He had learned the social skills of operating in a business environment. He seemed to know what to say at the right time and what not to say. He had a small family and a supporting wife who was the daughter of another prominent local businessman in the community. He had everything going for him.

Barry, on the other hand, was a farm boy. He had not had great training experiences. He was limited in experience because he never had tried to do anything other than helping his dad run the farm. He was a little awkward in knowing what to say in a given situation, and when not to talk at other times.

Although he was new in the business environment he somehow sensed that the things that he had learned on the farm could be adapted to his new occupation.

His old habits stayed with him. He was nearly always early arriving at the job and he immediately saw what needed to be done before the doors were opened to the public. And he did them immediately on arrival before anyone else got there.

When 5:00 in the afternoon came and everybody left to go home, he almost always stayed a little longer to clean up the place or to finish a job. When the work piled up at the end of the week, he often came in on Saturdays to help the boss clean up things that were left undone.

About a year passed and one day Chad confided in Barry that he was going to ask for a raise. Business was good and he thought that he could probably smooth-talk the old man out of some of the profits.

He was successful in getting his raise and he started taking home more money than Barry. He suggested to Barry that he too should ask for a raise. But Barry was born on a farm and was uncomfortable in asking to get more than some of the others workers. In his experience the harvest came and gave the workers what it wanted to give them. Sometimes they got a lot and sometimes just a little, but whatever it was they continued giving the potential crop their best effort.

Now the boss became so busy with the success of the business that he finally determined that he needed help. His wife told him that he needed to get an assistant. That made sense and it occurred to him that he had two good men in his organization to choose from.

Which one would he choose?
One was excellent in playing the **pull** game and the other one did his best at playing the **push** game. Which one would **you** choose?

Theadora was a school teacher. She had started out teaching the first grade students at the Eisenhower elementary school. And before she was thirty years old she was named the principal of the school.

Several teachers had applied for that position too and most had better credentials and more experience. Not everyone was happy with Theadora's promotion and that made her job all the more difficult. It was true that she made more money now with the new responsibility, but sometimes she thought the bigger job was not worth the bigger salary. But someone had to do it.

Theadora soon found that the educational system in her community was facing big problems. The problems were financial, racial, political and educational. No one seemed to have good answers and so life continued, but increasingly jumbled—chaotic and ominous.

The superintendent of schools, together with the school board, finally decided that a task force should be appointed to study the problems and make recommendations for solutions. Theadora was asked to be chairman of the task force of 20 teachers, administrators, community leaders, and students. She pondered long and hard as to what she should do. Advice came from many sources.

One, take the job and use it as a platform for a better position. The Superintendent was an older man and eligible for retirement. She could play her hand to get that job. The Superintendent's salary was double her principal salary, and it could be her's soon.

Two, she could accept a position on the task force, but decline the chairmanship, and recommend that Mr. Sawyer, the president of the local bank be chairman and that she would serve as his assistant.

What game has Theadora decided to play, **Push or Pull?** Which game **should** Theadora decide to play, **Push or Pull?**

Cindy is attractive, in fact she is the prettiest girl in her graduating class. As a senior who majored in business administration she will probably have no trouble in getting a job.

But she does have a problem. She has two young men who are both convinced that she should marry them. And they are both terrific individuals.

Kevin has a great future. He has majored in business and already his father wants him to come into his business. His father is president and owner of a manufacturing company that has had a long relationship with Ford Motor Company. The relationship has been an extremely profitable one and has allowed Kevin to enjoy the best of everything throughout his life.

In a few years it is expected that his father will leave the business to Kevin who is an only child. Money and opportunity will never be lacking if she were to marry Kevin, and he is so handsome.

Jeromy is also a real "catch." His father is a retired General which has allowed Jeromy to travel and live in numerous countries of the world. Jeromy has met the president of the United States and was once a visitor in the White House. He knows a bunch of movie stars and has already been offered a job in the office of a New York public relations firm.

Cindy is attracted to both young men and she has only a few weeks to make a decision. Her mother and father are no help to her at all. Her father is a preacher and told her to pray about it. Her mother just doesn't want to talk about it.

Cindy feels alone but yet invigorated by all of the possibilities that are in front of her. Heads, she wins. Tails, she wins. She just can't lose with the hand she is holding.

One night Cindy went out for a cup of coffee at the local diner. It was not a busy night and the owner of the cafe came over to talk to her. She chatted about her coming graduation and after three cups of coffee she told him of her quandary. He had no advice for her, only "You gotta do what you gotta do."

As she walked back to the dorm she wondered what on earth he meant. You gotta do what you gotta do.
She rebelled and said almost outloud, "I don't gotta do what I gotta do. I don't gotta do nothing and I'm not gonna do anything until I know more about life."

And at that moment she made a decision to accept the job as secretary in the United Way office in the small college town.

Did she make a mistake?

Will she regret not tossing a coin into the air and saying, "Heads I will marry Kevin. Tails I will marry Jeromy." And if it falls on the edge I will enjoy being a street person in a large rust-belt city anywhere that is not here.

But Cindy was too young to understand the **Push-Pull** game. She didn't know that some day she would be confronted by choosing between them and her choice would be the most important choice in her life.

Without knowing it, her choice to start out as a secretary in a United Way office was a major and good decision.

Why?

==========

Carmen Adams! Back to Carmen Adams. He is the one who gave me advice that has enriched my life in so many ways. Years later I received a letter in the mail and I opened it to find a generous check signed by Carmen Adams.

Did that mean that I had graduated into the **PUSH academy?** No, it was just the simple act of a good man who was following the game that **he chose.** I hadn't earned it. I was just the beneficiary of one who had chosen to live that way.

And I wonder what the world would be like if all of us would choose to play the **PUSH** game.

Would our schools be better if the teachers would play the **PUSH** game?

Would our families be better if mom and dad would play the **PUSH** game?

Would our businesses be better if management would play the **PUSH** game?

Would I, would you, be better off if we could become more adept at playing the **PUSH** game?

I wonder if the **Harvard Business School** could add this to their curriculum?

"Help others without any reason and give without the expectation of receiving anything in return."
— Roy T. Bennett

"We make a living by what we get. We make a life by what we give."
— Winston S. Churchill

"The most truly generous persons are those who give silently without hope of praise or reward."
— Carol Ryrie Brink,

"You can give without loving, but you can never love without giving."
— Robert Louis Stevenson

"Always give without remembering and always receive without forgetting."
— Brian Tracy

"You don't need much to give. Give what you have."
— Lailah Gifty Akita

"Real love never fails, never fades, and the greatest expression of it is giving."
— Gena Showalter

Companion Books in the
Win With Wisdom Series

"WISE Methods for WISE people"
Take Ten Steps to Reach Your Goals

Nearly everyone knows WHAT the goals are or WHAT they want. Few people know HOW to get the WHAT. A new movement has been formed to help people capture the skill of HOW to get things done, or as they call it how to **GTD**. This book is a primer or beginners guide. It is a road map which anyone can read or follow. It involves moving from a beginning point to a second point and then through eight other points which will help nearly anyone to GTD or arrive at a desirable destination.

Any reader who will invest 30 minutes of their time and $5) will be rewarded with a tool worth thousands of dollars and hours of new time.

"Save Yourselves with WISDOM"
How to avoid the Dangers of Tomorrow

Tomorrow will bring a cup of promise and a vat of dangers. No one will be exempt from either. The only solution is too get to know both and plan to avoid the dangers and profit from the promises.

Central to the book is a letter written by a wealthy tycoon to his wealthy clients. What he writes is appropriate   for the rich, and important for average families as well. To ignore his warnings would be sheer folly.

This book faces the warnings head-on and points to practical solutions. An investment of only 30 minutes of your time could be the best investment that you will make this year. The tycoons letter is a must-read.

"It's WISE To Know The Big Picture"
The strategies of *Getting by Giving*

This book is based on a story told by a very wealthy investor to an educator seeking a large financial gift. The educator received NO MONEY, but he was given a valuable secret that would always bring wealth to anyone brave enough to use it.

The book is small and only costs $5.00 and 30 minutes of your time, but you and the ones that you care about should have it. It could change your future.

"The WISDOM of Knowing yourself
and others"
Why you and others do what you do

Psychology has become one of the most popular studies in colleges and universities. Unfortunately it has been seized by the academicians who have morphed it into a complex tool, available only to the esoteric.

This book molds psychology into a useful every-day tool for average persons. There are no long words or complex formulas. The average person can use what he reads to understand himself and whose with whom he lives and works.

That it is a commonsense book for daily living is its merit. Don't show it to your professor, analyst or therapist. Read it yourself and use it daily.

"WISDOM on Fire"

It takes more than one stick to burn BIG

This small book is big on emotion, concepts and inspiration. It can be read in less than an hour, but it should be read only a few pages at a time.

And even if your memory is fading you will remember many phrases, sentences and passages for years to come. This book will be a unique experience. Don't miss it.

These books are all available from
Amazon.com.
Go to Amazon, and on Amazons search type:
Kenneth Shelby Armstrong Books. Select
the book that you want and pay Amazon.

To contact the author.
Kenneth Shelby Armstrong Th.D., Ed.D.
Email: KennethWrites@me.com
Phone: 1-580-873-2377
Address: 1036 Holiday Acres Drive
              Fort Towson, OK 74735

Now, take a few minutes
and look at some of the other books
that Dr. Armstrong has written.

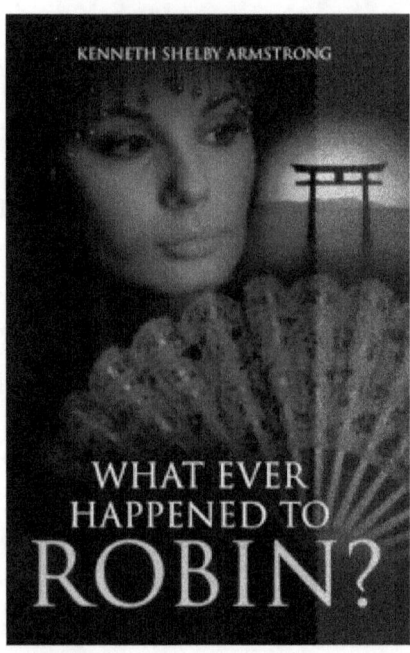

Whatever Happened To Robin?

Kenneth Shelby Armstrong
Publisher: Create Space
Available: Amazon or
Direct from Author
347 Pages
Copyright 2015

On the shores of Lake Biwa near Kyoto, Japan, a distinguished American bishop laid his head in the lap of a lovely Japanese woman and died. His death opened a secret that he had held since he was a young G.I. exploring the ruins of Hiroshima and Nagasaki with a young Japanese girl friend. The explosion of the secret shook a prominent American family and its church.

When he left Japan he promised to return and marry the girl of his dreams, but circumstances caused him to break that promise. Nevertheless, each New Year's Day he wrote her letters reaffirming his love and promising to return to her.

For decades he served his church as Bishop, but he never gave up his pledge to return to Robin. Nearing death he could delay no longer so he, used what strength he had to return to Japan and he laid his head in the lap of a lovely woman and died. But, to know the real secret you must read Whatever Happened to Robin?.

Who is more prejudiced?
White people or Black people

KENNETH SHELBY ARMSTRONG

Will It Be Dangerous? Could I Get Killed?

Kenneth Shelby Armstrong
Publisher: Create Space
Available: Amazon or
Direct from Author
129 Pages
Copyright 2015

"No! No! No You're looking at this thing all wrong. This will be a great educational experience. Just think of it! It's 1953 and segregation is the law of the State of Georgia and most other States in the South. A white graduate student walks into an all-negro University, say Atlanta University, and tries to enroll. What do you think would happen? This could be a life-changing experience for you, and it could bring about real change."

"That's what I'm thinking about. This life-changing experiment could get me killed. Have you ever heard of the Ku Klux Klan? If they hear about this I will be dead meat. If by some miracle the university should let me in, they will be breaking the law. It's illegal for them to accept a white student. I could even go to jail. I could get killed. And what if your Dean heard that you were advising one of your students to break the law? It could get you fired. But why should I worry? I'll be dead." The story of the book is, that I did get enrolled and I'm still alive and significantly more educated.

How To Strive, Thrive, And Stay Alive in Prison

Kenneth Shelby Armstrong
Publisher: Create Space
Available: Amazon or
Direct from Author
117 Pages
Copyright 2015

More than a million prisoners are now behind bars; eating three bland meals a day with never a change; each night they are serenaded by a chorus of snores from which there is no escape; they spend time in planning revenge on some member of their families or some policeman or judge who did them wrong; they wait for that special letter that never comes. Too often mail call is a downer. It's a tough life for the men, but much harder on the women.

Broken dreams become nightmares. Soft memories are crushed by harsh treatment from detention officials. Visiting hours are too brief and saying goodbye to family and small children erupts in tears that will continue for hours.

But some in prison find forgiveness and others discover that there is hope. Some discover beauty in unexpected places. Faith, hope, and love, live there too.

My Very Best Stories

Kenneth Shelby Armstrong
Publisher: Create Space
Available: Amazon or
Direct from Author
138 Pages
Copyright 2015

There is a really great editor/owner of the newspaper in the town where I live. He knows everybody and everybody knows him. In these days there are few towns and newspapers like the one we have in Hugo, Oklahoma. I read his editorials every day and hidden inside of each one is pungent information, sparkling humor, and honest concern for the town where he has lived all of his life, and which many of us have adopted.

Against all odds he has kept our newspaper something that we look forward to getting. One day he asked me to let him publish some of my short stories in the paper. I gladly accepted the assignment. It was so well received that we decided to publish those stories in a book. It's now available and the range of interest is broad enough to capture the interest of people even though they live in New York City or Los Angeles. These are stories for everyone.

I Was A Reluctant Guest
Kenneth Shelby Armstrong
Publisher: Create Space
Available: Amazon or
Direct from Author
236 Pages
Copyright 2015

Being in prison can be an exciting adventure. Every inmate has some great story to tell–and that over and over again. But the stories that come from prison are rooted in a minutia of facts, most of which are boring and void of meaning. The facts of each prisoner's case may be interesting only to a weird attorney or some other prisoner who is looking for some way to get out. What do you do when you are looking at twenty years in each dreadful place?

Of more interest than facts are the emotions and feelings alive in each prison. For the most part the emotions are kept within specifically prescribed boundaries, but too often they spill out like volcanic ash. The results can be fights, riots, and escapes. Neither guards nor reluctant guests look forward to such events. But you will begin to understand the drama of prison, inside and out.

He Died A Hero

Kenneth Shelby Armstrong
Publisher: Create Space
Available: Amazon or
Direct from Author
211 Pages
Copyright 2015

In our current culture a hero is someone, dressed in a cape and flying through the air with the greatest of ease to release some damsel who has gotten into the clutches of an ogre with warts. Of course the drama takes place on some remote planet located just above Kansas City. The plot is compelling and people will pay $15 just to experience the unreality of some weirdo's imagination.

On the other hand an unadorned reality is a country boy wearing patched overalls and sporting a straw hat with holes in the brim and a black sweat band earned while picking cotton under an Oklahoma sun, to earn a few cents to put bread on the table during the peak of the Great Depression. After supper he will study until his eye lids shut his brain down, but he is committed to getting a college education–the first in his family. With the diploma placed in the back pocket of his overalls he marched out to serve his God and those in need. What a Story!

> The two most
> important days in
> your life are the day
> you are born and the
> day you find out why.
>
> -Mark Twain